I0796362

Social Cinema: Opened in 1970, the *Filmhuset* building is home to the Swedish Film Institute, an icon of social democracy as applied to the silver screen. In the 1960s, film critic Harry Schein negotiated the Swedish Film Agreement with the government, leading to the foundation of the institute under shared ownership of the state, cinema proprietors and TV companies. Money from cinema tickets and other sources was plowed into home-grown productions. Today, Filmhuset is home to a giant cinema and a packed agenda of events. Beyond its brutalism, Peter Celsing's architecture has cute touches: the windows look like celluloid perforations, the building has the form of a camera, and from above it resembles a roll of film.

• Filmhuset (Swedish Film Institute), Östermalm, filminstitutet.se

Stockholm.

Beauty isn't just admired here, it's curated by an official Board of Beauty that ensures history and modernity exist in aesthetic harmony. Elegance is woven directly into the fabric of the North, but the city's charms extend beyond its tapestry of parks, islands and waterways. World-class culture thrives at every turn, from nearly a hundred museums and a three-star Michelin restaurant to groundbreaking designers who changed the way we decorate our homes. Swedish House Mafia, Alesso, Eric Prydz and Avicii have kept the world dancing long after ABBA's heyday, and behind the scenes, millennial-aged composer Ludwig Göransson already claims several Oscar, Emmy and Grammy wins, while Max Martin continues to write and produce a historic number of chart-topping hits.

Yet beyond the awards and accolades, it's the everyday people of Stockholm who truly define its character. In these pages, you'll meet the dreamers and doers who shaped its cultural landscape: the architect-turned-installation artist, the local DJ playing global stages, and the brothers who built a world-renowned photography museum. Through their stories, alongside curated recommendations, photographic essays and in-depth features, we invite you to experience the spirit and innovation of this beautiful archipelago city. Lose yourself in the sights, smells and flavors of the city. Get lost in Stockholm.

FILMHUSET
FILMHUSET
INSTITUTET
FER BAR & RESTAURANG

Outdoors **Aqua Vitae**

Swimming options abound in Stockholm, where it's legal to jump naked into any of the city's waters. *Eriksdalsbadet* has the largest pool around, while former prison isle Långholmen is beach-ringed and offers the chance to sleep in renovated cells. Sandy cove *Smedsuddsbadet* is the Stockholmers' family choice. But the classiest is the 1925-built wooden castle of *Saltsjöbadens Friluftsbad*. The open-air baths include one house for men and one for women—nudity embraced but not required—plus a mixed, clothed sandy beach and sauna with ice bath.
• Various locations, see Index, p.64

From Back-Pocket Dining to Naked Swimming

Northern Lights

Food **Pocket Gourmet**

The rise of Nordic cuisine introduced a fascinating side trend—the *bakficka* (back pocket) restaurant, where fine-dining chefs showcase their talents to a broader audience without the Michelin-star price tag. For instance, the two-star *Aloë* extends its creativity to *Black Milk Gastro Bar* (pictured), a sister restaurant that effortlessly shifts from sunny Mediterranean lunches to Japanese omakase dinners. Similarly, Sweden's only three-star chef, Björn Frantzén, transformed a 19th-century theater into *Brasserie Astoria*, a glamorous 1920s-style eatery where table-side preparations add to the spectacle.
• Various locations, see Index, p.64

Photos: 1) Henrik Trygg, 2) Erik Olsson Photography, 3) Black Milk Gastro Bar

Culture Photo Bomb

Fotografiska, housed in an Art Nouveau customs house on the waterfront, celebrates photographic art on its century-old walls. The museum opened in 2010 with an Annie Leibovitz retrospective, setting the tone for dynamic exhibitions by the likes of provocateur Robert Mapplethorpe and local talent like Klara Källström and Helena Blomqvist. The top-floor restaurant, which earned a Michelin Green Star for its commitment to sustainability, enjoys sweeping harbor views framed in its floor-to-ceiling windows. Fotografiska has since opened sister locations worldwide and merged with the coworking company NeueHouse, establishing the museum as a creative hub for artistic expression.

• Fotografiska, Södermalm, fotografiska.eu

Shop | Masters of Décor

Everyone is talking about Scandinavian fashion, but long before their threads became famous the Swedish were crafting era-defining furniture. *Jacksons* (pictured) is perhaps the foremost temple of Nordic interior design. Paul and Carina opened their first gallery in 1981 and have since added considerably to their treasure trove, often exhibiting at international design fairs. Their Stockholm space in Östermalm (there's an outpost in Berlin, too) is a key stop for lovers of beauty. If you fancy taking something home, be prepared to drop a small fortune: otherwise simply enjoy exquisite exhibitions, like the recent "Nordic Modernism," as you furnish your imaginary dream house. In the same neighborhood, Viennese elegance and Swedish functionalism meet at *Svenskt Tenn*, where the collection remains influenced by the ideals of founding duo Estrid Ericson and Josef Frank. Whether you have space in your suitcase and on your credit card, it's worth a look—and a cultured refreshment stop in the Tea Room.

• Various locations, see Index, p.64

Food | Stock Market

Stockholm offers a market experience for every taste. Watch celebrated chefs reinvent comfort food at *Teatern*, the Södermalm food court with charcoal-grilled Korean tacos at *Nū* and Japanese noodles from Michelin-starred chefs at *Raamen*. Find more global flavors at *Hötorgshallen* in Norrmalm, where Lebanese hummus goes toe to toe with Swedish herring. For a taste of classic Scandinavia, step back in time at *Östermalms Saluhall*, a 19th-century market with local delicacies like game, cheese and artisanal sausages, or even grab a bite at *Lisa Elmqvist* (pictured), a seafood institution since 1926.

• Various locations, see Index, p.64

Photos: 1) Lindman Photography, 2) Provided by Lisa Elmqvist, 3) Charlie Bennet 4) Musikaliska

Outdoors · Culture | Outsider Art

Shrouded by pine trees on the island of Värmdö, *Artipelag* is just 20 minutes from Stockholm center. Eschew the roads in favor of a boat: sailing into the heart of the archipelago is an experience, chiming with the gallery's credo of combining art and nature. Johan Nyrén's magnificent building covers over ten thousand square meters, and hosts a broad range of exhibitions, showcasing artists from Tracey Emin to Candida Höfer. But the oeuvre isn't limited to the walls—rising through the floor of the café is a two-billion-year-old metamorphic gneiss rock, and the surrounding views and boardwalks speak for themselves.

• Artipelag, Värmdö, artipelag.se

Night | Norrmalm Sounds

Some of Stockholm's best beats are to be found in the unlikeliest of places. Within a stunning 19th-century concert hall in Norrmalm, follow the noise to a stylish bar (pictured). Take your cocktail outside to the courtyard, and surprise: you'll be serenaded by underground DJs from all over Europe. This is *Musikaliska Kvarteret*, an utterly Stockholm experience best enjoyed during warm, promising nights. A nearby all-weather alternative lies in the underbelly of the iconic *Berns*. The luxury hotel hosts two nightclubs, with *LE!* spinning EDM and house music while *NEU* delivers more hard techno. Both spots feature a proper club vibe with lights, lasers and one of the best sound systems in Scandinavia.

• Various locations, see Index, p.64

Photo: © Anna Kleberg

Jonas Dahlberg

The victims of Norway's brutal Utøya massacre on July 22, 2011, received a spectacular commemoration from artist Jonas Dahlberg—who proposed to cut out an entire chunk from an island. The Swede is also known for installing cameras in toilets to question our age of surveillance, filming empty cities to address ignored populations and launching other captivating projects that stem from his architectural roots and unique spatial perspective

Jonas Dahlberg, Artist

Visible City

Though Stockholm might not be present in much of his work, Jonas Dahlberg's work is definitely present in Stockholm—in the form of a permanent sound installation at the KTH School of Architecture and ongoing exhibitions in local museums and galleries. Here, Dahlberg talks about the relationship between artist and city, takes us to a peaceful refuge and even tells us what to watch to enter a Stockholm state of mind

Sharp edges and sharper art on display at Galleri Riis in Norrmalm

Some of your work investigates the world's overlooked cities. Is Stockholm one?

No, not really. With the "Invisible Cities" project, I reflected that we often speak of mega-cities that generate new conditions and problems for urban living, and sometimes of rural areas and their depopulation—but that we rarely talk of the in-between cities where a large part of the world's population lives. The parameters I set for an Invisible City was that its population should be between ten thousand and one hundred thousand people. So Stockholm, with around a million inhabitants, does not qualify.

You're often cited as one of Sweden's most prominent artists, especially since you won the competition to make Norway's July 22 memorial. How has Europe's political climate affected your art?

There's no easy answer to this. But lately I've been occupied with thinking about public space and its politics, and how it functions within a society. The way we live with each other and share or don't share spaces—or are even unwilling to share spaces with others who are not like us.

If Stockholm were a person, would you get along?

I don't get along with so many people and I am afraid that Stockholm is sometimes one of them.

What's a typical Sunday in town for you?

Photo: 1) Jean-Baptiste Beranger, 2) erik olsson photography

An award-winning international art bookstore: Konst-ig merchandises their shelves with titles on architecture, art, design, fashion, graphic design and photography

Lundbergs Konditori
Södermalm

Bar Hommage
Södermalm

Gamla Amsterdam
Södermalm

Konst-ig
Södermalm

Any day can turn out to be a Sunday just as much as it can turn out to be a Monday. But whatever day of the week it is, I like to start my day with a coffee in my neighborhood at *Lundbergs Konditori*.

Where do you go for a relaxed drink or to celebrate good news?

For drinks there's a nice bar, *Hommage*.

Where would you stock up on delicacies?

I buy cheese at *Gamla Amsterdam* on Södermalm. It's a lovely little place.

Is there any particular place in the city that never fails to inspire you?

I don't really get so inspired by cities. Many of my ideas actually come when I'm in the summer cabin on Valö island in the archipelago—outside Fjällbacka on the west coast of Sweden. But one thing I really love about Stockholm is its proximity to nature. I'm aware that this is a very Swedish thing to list as one of the major qualities of a city.

Stockholm has a fantastic selection of paper and bookshops. Where do you stock up?

At the bookstore *Konst-ig* in Södermalm or when I'm in New York.

Your work shows your roots in architecture. Is there a specific building in the city you feel an attachment to?

The *Skogskyrkogården* cemetery by Gunnar Asplund and Sigurd Lewerentz. So special, beautiful and cinematic.

Skogskyrkogården
Söderort

Galleri Riis
Norrmalm

Galerie Nordenhake
Östermalm

What are your favorite galleries? Any artists you're excited about?

Galleri Riis works with Kristina Matousch and Christina Ödlund. The gallery also works with another artist doing great work, Lisa Tan. I should probably mention I live with Lisa, so I am a bit biased. But in the spirit of being blatantly partial, I'll also mention *Galerie Nordenhake* —the gallery in Stockholm I work with. The director Ben Loveless always picks up interesting artists and puts together great shows.

You've also relied heavily on film as a medium for your art; could you tell us a bit about the Swedish film landscape?

I have to admit that I am not so up-to-date on contemporary Swedish film. But I recently saw a few episodes of *The Mind of a Chef* about Swedish chef Magnus Nilsson and his restaurant Fäviken. Maybe that could be interesting to see before visiting Sweden. And also the Norwegian film *Insomnia* from 1997, with Swedish actor Stellan Skarsgård. It'll lend an understanding of the bright summer nights and what that can do to the psyche. And for the winter variation, just close your eyes and imagine them staying closed for four months....

Any favorite music stores in town? What are you listening to at the moment?

Music stores I stopped visiting many years ago... I live happily together with Spotify. But Spotify is Swedish, so maybe that counts as my choice of a Stockholm music store. I have been working on an architectural project in Bristol in collaboration with Populous and Feilden, Clegg, Bradley architects, so to get in the right mood in the studio I have been listening to the Bristol bands Portishead and Massive Attack.

And what does the music to accompany Stockholm sound like?

I would say that the new Anna von Hausswolff album, *The Miraculous*, is a pretty good soundtrack to Stockholm in the winter.

A lot of Sweden's big artists are working in cities like Berlin and New York—and you have had periods of working from abroad. How would you explain this creative brain drain?

Because Stockholm is an expensive city. Because people feel constrained by the culture that they grew up in. Because it is too clean and organized. Because people do not greet each other on the streets or smile at each other.

And, inversely, why Stockholm?

Because we have a good support system for artists for now. Because you know the system and culture you grew up in, so you're left to focus on other things. Because it is clean and organized. Because it is nice not to feel the need to greet people on the streets with a hi and a smile.

Photo: Skogskyrkogården / Stockholm Media Bank

Skogskyrkogården cemetery was designed to depict the changing character of Nordic architecture

Södermalm & Söderort

Song of the South

Stockholm's bohemian heartland, the neighborhood of Södermalm, is so frothing with art, fashion and food that some feel "Söder" has gone too far. What remains but to keep pushing southward into Söderort—to stay ahead of the gentrification wave

Shop **Capital of Cool**

Söder pulses with innovation in the fashion realm—so reserve time to get through its stores. To blend in with stylish Stockholmers, make institution *Grandpa* (pictured) your first stop. The concept store displays a mix of apparel, paper goods and design objects. Environmental awareness is important in Sweden. It's been successfully incorporated by labels like *Nudie Jeans* and *Deadwood Studios*, both with flagship stores on eco-chic Söder. The former focuses on sustainable denim, while the latter is all about ultra-smart, upcycled biker jackets. Nearby is *Nitty Gritty* with a selection of smart streetwear labels like APC and Commes des Garçons. Also on Söder can be found two branches of *Aplace*, a chain with its own magazine and an edgy, curated blend of international and local labels, including Wood Wood, Norse Projects and Acne. Meanwhile, vintage lovers can find everything on the island, from archival designer pieces to 1990s casualwear. A pick is *POP Stockholm*, embracing Woodstock 1969 with its Americana vintage. Looking for inspiration? Head to *Papercut* for a handpicked selection of books and magazines on fashion, design, art and travel.

• Various locations, see Index, p.64, Södermalm

Photos: 1) Grandpa, 2) Dusty Deco, 3) Carla Orrego Veliz, 4) Jakob Fridholm

Shop **Curiosity Cabinet**

Just by a popular bar street in Hornstull, a mysterious door leads to a space sprinkled with curious objects. The owners of *Dusty Deco* scout treasures from all around the world and bring old industrial design, exotic taxidermy, massive furniture and unusual photography to their storage space. Rough and kitschy might be the best way to define Dusty Deco's style—with everything from whale bone sculptures and mushroom specimens to a leather divan that seems to remember Uncle Freud.

• Dusty Deco, Linnégatan 13, Östermalm, dustydeco.com

Food **Vantastic**

For a quick refreshment stop in Stockholm's hippest zone, treat yourself to a real local delicacy: fried herring. The one offered at the humble-looking food truck outside Slussen metro station has gained legendary status. *Nystekt Strömming* is the perfect spot to enjoy the midnight sun or a wintry night—or to satisfy a post-party craving for street food. Summon your inner Swede and choose the traditional version on hard rye bread, or go for the fast food twist: a pita wrap stuffed with herring and mashed potatoes.

• Nystekt Strömming, Kornhamnstorg 1, Galma Stan

Food **East Meets North**

Formerly of Gothenburg's legendary Kock & Vin, and via a turn at Stockholm's Flying Elk, chef Claes Grännsjö uses his Korean roots to infuse Nordic dishes with an Asian touch at *Nook*. The décor evokes Söder's zeitgeist with industrial walls, checkered flooring and vintage chairs, but it's the creative cuisine at reasonable prices that pulls in the clientele. Offered two set menus at differing price points, diners have the opportunity to try delights like roast lamb with beets, goat's cheese, aubergine, wild garlic and capers.

• Nook, Åsögatan 176, Södermalm, nookrestaurang.se

Culture · Night **Color Factory**

The industrial area of Liljeholmen is a booming spot on Söder's map. It's close to the central attractions, yet far enough away to be fertile ground for underground initiatives. *Färgfabriken* (Color Factory, pictured) is a contemporary art hall set in the spacious interior of a former munitions plant. In the summer and between exhibitions, it turns into a lively clubbing space. Among its events, look out for "Natten," a party dedicated to slow dancing. Weekends offer brunch and Thursdays host an evening flea market.
• Färgfabriken, Lövholmsbrinken 1, Södermalm, fargfabriken.se

Shop **Second Life**

When the well-dressed denizens of Stockholm freshen up their wardrobes, there's one place where their older beloved garments are sure to get a new lease on life. *Judits* is a vintage shop that demands time to leisurely peruse season-appropriate items displayed with love. Vintage gems from the 1950s to 1970s share a well-decorated home with an assortment of designer duds. From an antique cocktail dress to a vintage Miu Miu brooch or Louis Vuitton tote, Judits will hold something for most fashion lovers among its racks.
• Judits, Hornsgatan 75, Södermalm, judits.se

Shop · Food **In the Hood**

Escape the crowds and discover the charming tranquility of Midsommarkransen, a hidden gem just south of Södermalm. This residential neighborhood is lined with local shops that reflect its bohemian spirit. Looking for something special? Find handcrafted, bespoke lamps at *2 Little Spoons*, alongside a curated selection of quirky crafts from boutique artisan designers. Once you've scored a few unique finds, unwind next door at *Gaia Matbar* (pictured), a Swedish bistro serving natural wine, crisp local ciders and a fearless menu filled with inventive flavors.
• Various locations, see Index, p.64, Söderort

Photos: 1) Ake E. Son Lindman, 2) Carla Orrego Veliz, 3) Gaia Matbar, 4) Konsthall C

Culture · Food

Social Suburbia

For pockets of rich culture, it helps to move a little further out. A short 20-minute journey on the lavishly decorated metro from downtown Stockholm takes you southward—and back in time—to Hökarängen. The area was used in the 1960s as an experimental neighborhood for the *Folkhemmet* (people's home) concept of harmonious communal living during Sweden's social democratic heyday. And a key reminder of those times is *Konstall C* (pictured). The former public laundry has been revived to serve its communal purposes once again. As well as reopening the washing facilities, artist Per Hasselberg and his community acquired the space to present interdisciplinary art projects in a post-industrial setting. Most of the main shows are politically minded, while a smaller space called Centrifug holds separate exhibitions. Open the door on the right to see a collection of old washing machines and mangles. If Swedish artistic and political consciousness summons an appetite, head to nearby Hökarängsplan, the country's first pedestrian-only street, for Swedish-Mediterranean fusion at *Kollektivet* and strong Colombian coffee next door at *Kaffé Express Colombia*. If you're there as darkness falls, you'll see the neighborhood lit up by the glow of neon signs.

• Various locations, see Index, p.64, Söderort

Jan & Per Broman, Curators

Developing Scene

Jan & Per Broman
Jan and Per Broman grew up in Salem, Sweden. After years following their own paths, they came together to rekindle a 70-year-old dream for an all-encompassing photography space in Sweden. Beyond Fotografiska's four unique exhibitions a year and a range of smaller shows, the space provides courses, concerts and conferences too. The award-winning restaurant offers one of the city's finest panoramic views

Brothers Jan and Per Broman founded Fotografiska in 2010, now one of the most spectacular, forward-thinking art hubs in Scandinavia. Feeling at home in the city where "everything works," the Bromans name-drop some upcoming photographers and discuss sea changes in the al fresco dining scene as Stockholm shakes off some of its historic government restrictions

Photo: Knut Koivisto

Fotografiska
Södermalm

Larsen Warner
Östermalm

Andréhn-Schiptjenko
Östermalm

Anna Bohman Gallery
Östermalm

Starting with photography, are there any upcoming Swedish snappers we should look out for?

Per: The circle of brilliant photographers in Sweden just keeps on growing. Many are young women—Helena Blomqvist, Nygårds Karin Bengtsson, Helene Schmitz and Maria Friberg, to name a few—they are all very talented.

What makes Stockholm special for you?

Jan: I've always lived in Stockholm. I always traveled a lot, but I always came back. It's a small city, extremely beautiful, with helpful people—and everything works. That's the foundation of why I love to live in Stockholm. In the last five, six years—not just in Stockholm, but also in Sweden, Norway, Denmark—the food scene has exploded. Ten years ago you really had to know where to go for a decent meal. But today you can pop into almost any restaurant. It's a little bit like Italy I would say, that you almost can pop in everywhere, if you exclude the Chinese and Indian restaurants and the pizza places. *Fotografiska* has been a trendsetter for the new scene in which fish and meat are no longer key to the meal; it's vegetables which are the key, and then you can add the fish and meat. That's exploding now since we opened, so the scene for vegetarians is fantastic today.

What other places would you recommend?

Jan: Because I'm so busy all the time, I'm not the best one to say what's good or not.

Are there other ways in which Stockholm has changed?

Jan: There has been an explosion of outdoor serving, that's to say places to eat or drink outside. This was legally restricted in the past and the change has given Stockholm a much more continental feeling. The laws have loosened up over the past five, six years. Compared to Europe it's still very strict, but we have a sort of relationship which works now.

Are there things Stockholm does better than anywhere else?

Per: We are very free with all the water, which makes Stockholm a beautiful city, and then it's also clean, and almost everything works. If somebody says they will open up 9am, they will open up at 9am—that's a big difference to a lot of other cities around the world.

Aside from Fotografiska, where is good for an art fix in Stockholm?

Jan: If you're into art, there are a few great galleries near each other that are part of a good contemporary Swedish art scene. You can find *Larsen Warner* gallery and the *Andréhn-Schiptjenko* gallery. Also one of my favorite galleries in the *Anna Bohman Gallery*—not far from the cluster of galleries around there.

You've said Stockholm's one of the world's most beautiful cities. Where are the best photo spots?

Per: I would say the Fotografiska restaurant has one of the most beautiful views, because you can see all the Old Town and Skeppsholmen island—everything is in a fantastic spot from there with the water in the front.

Jan: And of course the street Fjällgatan, just up from us. People from Stockholm always claim that's the best view of the city. And Mariaberget on Södermalm is another fantastic vantage point looking over the city.

The Larsen Warner gallery is a contemporary art gallery with an extensive international program

Cadier Bar at Grand Hotel
Norrmalm

Lydmar Hotel
Norrmalm

Strandvägen 1
Östermalm

Mister French
Gamla Stan

Spritmuseum
Djurgården

Debaser
Södermalm

Pelikan
Södermalm

What's the best way to survive the Stockholm winter?

Jan: Really good clothing and fantastic shoes, because it's wet in the winter. And in terms of where to hide out, I love *Cadier Bar* at *Grand Hotel*. The *Lydmar Hotel* also has a fantastic bar with great food as well. And I'd recommend the restaurant *Strandvägen 1* as a great place to go to.

What would be your tipple at the Grand Hotel bar?

Jan: I'm a gin-tonic guy, so I'd go with that.

How about the best way to make the most of the summer?

Per: Summer I would say *Mister French*, a fantastic bar with an outdoor spot next to the water. And of course our outdoor serving at Fotografiska.

Jan: *Spritmuseum* (Spirit Museum) is also great. You don't realize you're in the city when you're at their outdoor area, because the city seems so far away. But you're in the center still.

Do you enjoy live music or DJs? Where do you go for your music fix?

Jan: I go to the *Debaser* to listen to music. Could be anything from reggae to hard rock.

What about for traditional Swedish food?

Jan: Personally I'd never go for that, but *Pelikan* is the place for it. The ambiance is much better than the menu, but … that's an old style of Swedish food.

Per: Also, the restaurant *Riche* serves the most delicious meatballs. It's one of the best meeting places in Stockholm.

The Swedes are known as the "Japanese of the North"—test the comparison at Japanese-style open-air spa Yasuragi

Riche
Östermalm

Yasuragi
Hasseludden

Vasa Museum
Djurgården

Skansen Museum
Djurgården

Do you know a good relaxing spot for a trip outside the city?

Per: I'd recommend *Yasuragi*, a Japanese-inspired spa a few miles outside Stockholm. The year before Fotografiska opened we spent many hours in the baths at Yasuragi, planning our big opening.

What would you say is an absolute must for visitors?

Jan: If you're here in the summertime, go by the boats out to the archipelago one day at least. Twenty minutes after leaving the city center, the archipelago starts and it's amazing scenery. There's 25,000 islands.

Per: You have the *Vasa Museum* if you're into old boats, that's one of the few things which is totally unique for Stockholm. And then you have *Skansen*, an outdoor museum with old houses and animals of the Nordic region—a perfect spot if you're here with kids. Other than that, just stroll around, walk a lot and have a fika and a glass of wine in the afternoon.

And finally, where would you like to see Stockholm in ten years' time?

Jan: I would demand more control of the outdoor scene from the government. I think that's the most important thing to change. We could use outdoor spaces for serving alcohol and food in a better way, with longer hours.

Per: We're so restricted when it comes to the alcohol part of it. That's how it works in Sweden, but I think it has to change to bring a much more continental feeling to the city. But overall Stockholm is a fantastic place to visit and live in.

Echoes of Design

Alice Ulvsgärd

Josef Frank and Estrid Ericson, designer and founder, respectively, of Svenskt Tenn, one of Stockholm's premier interior design stores. Svenskt Tenn celebrated its one hundredth anniversary in 2024

"Stockholm moves like this. Between worlds. Between times. Design is not just aesthetics but generations speaking to each other. You see it in the windows of antique shops, in the hushed conversations at Nordiska Galleriet where collectors circle the latest revival, waiting to claim a piece of history as their own. Objects live; they do not die. They shift and they evolve. They breathe new life into old rooms."

I stand in my grandmother's apartment; the air feels thick with the weight of time. The light plays through the lace curtains, casting restless shadows over furniture that was once just that, furniture. Now, they are relics and trophies, objects that tell stories. My grandmother, a collector. She was. Pieces piled on every surface, dark mahogany next to lacquered pine, Josef Frank's iconic florals clashing against raw metal and the shine of Skultuna's polished brass. It is a lived-in chaos. So many things, yet so much space. Death lingers close by, but the room pulses with life. The sunlight hits the floor lamp that sighs softly; *where are we now*, it asks aloud.

Maybe we are in the 1930s. A man in a linen suit leans over a drafting table at Svenskt Tenn, watercolor bleeding into paper, his hands shaping the future with swirling botanical patterns. Or maybe we are in the 1970s, when a woman lounges on a brown corduroy sofa, swearing that *this is a classic*, that *this is forever.* Or maybe we are right here, in this very moment, as I scan the room, feeling the shapes press in around me. The armchair catches my eye, the one my grandmother once found in the trash and had reupholstered in Frank's fabric. *Disgusting*, I remember thinking back then. But here it is, still standing. A shape I see everywhere today. Proof that no idea is never truly new, just reimagined.

Her home feels like a portal, a world where time collapses into one. And maybe that is exactly what Stockholm is, a city of past and future entwined. A place where people chase not just beauty but stories. What people want is just that: the creaky floors, the century-old crown moldings, the craftsmanship, like it is the proof of something real.

The crackle of an old radio lingers in the background, a soft hum of a distant melody. I imagine my grandmother stepping into the room, holding the most spring-like branches. Carefully she places them in the small vase held by the Liljan candleholder from Skultuna. A birthday gift, once new, now eternal. I blink, and the branches are gone, but the vase remains, standing atop a pile of old issues of *FORM* magazine. The brass catches the light from the window, gleaming, alive. The top drawer of the cabinet opens. *Help yourself*, it says. Exactly like my grandmother would have said. I stand up. The silver glows dimly in the corner, grasping the last ray of afternoon light. I wonder how many hands have polished it, admired its weight and let their fingers trace the cold curves of its form. My grandmother's, my mother's, mine. A century passes in a second. I slip the bracelet on my wrist, next to the one from All Blues, both pieces speaking the same language of form and craftsmanship, just in different accents. Fashion, like interior design, two worlds that work the same way, a constant cycle with shapes that reappear as new. A dialogue between generations, a pulse that keeps beating through time. Sunlight hits the floor lamp, and its shade flickers awake. *Are we back in the 1930s*, it asks again. How would I know?

Josef Frank looks up from his drafting table, the brush still wet in his hand and the pea green watercolor pooling on the paper. Outside, birds are singing their spring melody. He tilts his head, considering the balance of color, of movement, of life. My hand swipes over the lampshade, dust crumbling between my fingers. The paint bleeds into the transparent paper, swirling into life. He does not know yet that these patterns will still be here in a hundred years, that a woman in another time will run her hands over them and wonder what is the past and what is the present. Or maybe he does know. Maybe he glances up for a second, sensing something, a presence, time folding in on itself. A scene that fades as I look at the same pattern covering a lampshade in my grandmother's living room.

I sit down in the armchair, the same one that once belonged to my grandmother. I think of my mother's brown corduroy sofa, a piece that was passed down from my grandmother and became an untouchable relic. We could never change it, they said. *It is a classic*. But to me? It was ugly. Heavy. Outdated. Proof that we had got it wrong in comparison to the light, minimalistic Scandinavian designs my friends had. Simplicity, and everything white. I was embarrassed. The cluttered home. The mix of styles. The deep woods, the fabrics stacked on each other. But now I see it. Pieces that were classics, that still are today.

Classic. The world itself is a paradox. Something that stands forever, yet is constantly reinterpreted. The quiet perfection of old craftsmanship, passed down through generations. Pieces that are found in places like Svenskt Tenn, Nordiska Galleriet, and Skultuna, where the richness and warmth of well-made objects form homes that do not just look good in a magazine but live, breathe, and tell stories.

Today, that old sofa? It is iconic. The chaos of my childhood home, the cluttered beauty, is exactly what people are after now. The depth. The history. The personality. This is Scandinavian design as I know it.

Outside, Stockholm is waking up. I walk with my mother through the cobblestone streets of Strandvägen, the cool spring air biting my skin. People are out, talking, walking. The city is alive. Boats pass along the water; glasses clink from a nearby café. We are on our way to Svenskt Tenn after seeing the one hundredth anniversary exhibition at Liljevalchs. Built in the early 1900s, Liljevalchs is Stockholm's first independent art gallery, a meeting place for new ideas where past and future collide in curated exhibitions that push boundaries. The building itself is tucked into Djurgården, a nature-filled oasis in the middle of the city.

We climb the staircase and step into a recreated studio of Estrid Ericson, the founder of Svenskt Tenn. Styled exactly as it was when she worked here, with pewter objects scattered across the desk and personal items filling the shelves. She is here. Lifting a candleholder, weighing it in her hand as she searches for inspiration among her objects. The moment stretches, then snaps back. I blink, and I am standing in the same space, holding a candleholder. I turn it over, feeling its weight. I imagine my children finding it in my home one day, perhaps hating it but later coming to love it as I do.

After a short walk and a traditional herring lunch in the newly renovated Östermalms Saluhall, I step into Nordiska Galleriet. A place where the past is not past at all but continuously reinterpreted. Bruno Mathsson's chairs sit next to sculptural pieces, raw-edged marble tables and the bold geometry of Dusty Deco's Arco lounge chair. A couple walks slowly through the showroom, running their hands along the curved lines of an armchair. It is my favorite piece at home, Elias Svedberg's armchair by Dusty Deco. A classic, but with a twist of a zebra-patterned fabric. It speaks to me and fits my home today, as the same chair, upholstered differently, fits my grandmother's. The same comfort, but something else.

Stockholm moves like this. Between worlds. Between times. Design is not just aesthetics but generations speaking to each other. You see it in the windows of antique shops, in the hushed conversations at Nordiska Galleriet where collectors circle the latest revival, waiting to claim a piece of history as their own. Objects live; they do not die. They shift and they evolve. They breathe new life into old rooms.

I see it now. Where the classics are pulled from obscurity, reimagined and reborn. Where the techniques used centuries ago are still at play, shaping new forms and speaking to new generations. In my own home with the mess I once hated, the curated chaos. The old sofa that I never understood. Now I chase it; now everyone does. Because design is not about the present or about the past. It is about what happens in between. A cycle. A pulse. Waiting to be seen, to catch the light, to speak again. A dialogue that never really ends. Maybe that is why I am drawn to these pieces now. Not just for their beauty, but for their weight. The stories they carry and the history they hold. The candleholder that will outlive me. The pattern that has survived a century. Swedish design is not about keeping the past alive or creating something entirely new. It is about this. This cycle of revival. And in that, there is something timeless.

I lean back in my grandmother's armchair. The weight of history presses against my spine, not heavy, not outdated, but grounding. The objects around me, once too much, too chaotic, whisper something different now. This curated mess. This layered life. This is what we are chasing. Not trends, but stories. They are suddenly here, back again.

Writer: Alice Ulvsgärd is a designer and creative, from an island in the archipelago of Stockholm, now based in Mallorca. Alice works across visual design, photography and copywriting.

Image: Photograph by John Kjellstrom (1921-1995), March 22, 1952, Stockholm City Museum, Photo number SvD 36680

Klara Källström & Thobias Fäldt, Photographers & Publishers

Off Book

Klara Källström & Thobias Fäldt

Klara Källström's globe-roving photography has earned her prominence in the Swedish art scene—and an installation in the Stockholm Subway. Meanwhile Thobias Fäldt is the only photographer with two Scanpix photo awards under his belt—thanks to a knack for lesser-explored points of view. Together "KK+TF" are co-founders of art publisher B-B-B-Books, boldly going for topics like Julian Assange in exile and the 2011 Athens protests

While Klara Källström and Thobias Fäldt might roam from San Francisco to Shanghai in search of photographic spoils, they always bring them back to Stockholm's placid waterways and hidden corners. Here, they tell us where to find a rare vintage book or have a candlelit dinner for two, and share details of artist communities and local bands not to be missed

"The Artist's Bar"—Konstnärsbaren's environment is characterized by murals covering the dining room walls

Årstaviken/Tanto Strandbad
Södermalm

Glenn Miller Café
Norrmalm

Rönnell's Antikvariat
Norrmalm

Zita
Norrmalm

Bio Rio
Södermalm

Orionteatern
Södermalm

What's your neighborhood like?

Klara: We live on one of the main streets of Södermalm, Folkungagatan. It's quite lively, full of cheap—for Stockholm—bars and restaurants of all sorts.

What does the perfect Sunday include?

Thobias: A walk around Söder along *Årstaviken* is something that we do quite a lot. It's a beautiful city to take walks in.

What places are shaping Stockholm's artists today? Any new names you're excited about?

Klara: Stockholm has a lot of venues that have been around for many years, and play an important role in the culture scene: the jazz café *Glenn Miller*, the antique bookstore *Rönnells*, the cinemas *Zita* and *Bio Rio* and the theater *Orionteatern*. Since the larger art institutions are all based here, there is a big influx of international artists.

Thobias: Other interesting things happen in the communities of artists forming their own centers. Their activities take place wherever there are vacant spaces: in theaters, offices, antique shops and so on. Some examples are the music label Repeat Until Death, the filmmaker duo MDEMC and filmmaker and writer Johannes Wahlström. When you visit Stockholm, look out for gigs by the fantastic bands Tross,

Pelikan
Södermalm

Stockholms
Fotoantikvariat
Södermalm

Antikvariat
Mullvaden
Södermalm

Dovas Bar
Södermalm

Östgötakällaren
Södermalm

Konstnärsbaren
Norrmalm

Fiskjägarna and Fire! Orchestra—they're not to be missed!

Where do you typically take friends who come to visit?

Klara: We usually go to any of the SARA restaurants that still remain in the city. SARA stands for *Stockholms Allmänna Restaurangaktiebolag*—those restaurants (e.g., Pelikan) used to be run by the state due to the alcohol restrictions. Back in the old days, these places served affordable food and were open to everyone. These days, at least much of the interiors are intact and the atmosphere is nice. The prices have changed a lot though.

Tell us about the process behind your publishing house?

Thobias: For B-B-B-Books we collaborated with the design duo 1:2:3, Axel Von Friesen and Petter Törnqvist. We decided to set up a publishing house to create the kind of publications we wanted, without having to compromise.

Klara: For us the book is the reason. We come to the result through a collaborative process, meaning the books cannot be reduced to the sum of their parts. Each new book is a contribution to the collection of thoughts and common milieu in which our projects can live.

Thobias: There's always a moment in our collaborative process when "the other" has reshaped the initial idea to the point where things are not especially comfortable anymore. We've learned to appreciate this time of crisis within the project. To leave this comfort zone has become crucial to the process. This involves a lot of trust between all of us.

Where do you get your supplies for work? Are there other good places for book shopping?

Thobias: If you're looking for rare books, just walk to *Mullvaden*.

Where do you guys go for a drink or to unwind after a long day?

Klara: We usually call our friend who lives next to *Dovas Bar* and we meet there. The crowd is mixed and the staff are friendly. The favorite spot, though, is *Östgötakällarn*. They had this brilliant idea of lowering the price of beer after 10pm. The staff are fantastic and the interior is interesting.

And when it's time for a romantic dinner out?

Thobias: We go to *Konstnärsbaren*, KB, in Östermalm. They serve classic home-cooked food and the murals are beautiful. The bar is great as well.

You travel a lot for work—what do you miss about Stockholm when you're away?

Klara: This is a beautiful city and it's very nice to take long walks in Stockholm. The thing we miss the most when we are away is the accessibility to the water.

And what don't you miss about it? What would you like to see happen in Stockholm in the future?

Thobias: For it to be easier for those who make interesting things to show them in spaces for many people to see. It's a rather closed city, and we wish it would open up to more of what the people from this place have to offer.

A 1940s single-screen cinema features at Bio Rio, along with a range of cultural offerings and a restaurant

Wish You Were Here

Joakim Kocjancic

Rendering ambiguous scenes in black and white, Kocjancic's photographs are a tribute to the poetry of reality. His style is instinctual and reactive—for him, a way of understanding the enigma of life and creating a tangible connection to situations before him. This showcase is a continuation of his photo book *Paradise Stockholm*

Mikael Einarsson
Mikael Einarsson is the chef that almost never was. After high school, he went against his passion to study economics. After a year, he corrected that mistake to become a chef, and what a successful journey that's become. He's led top restaurants like Djuret, Leijontornet and Brasserie Astoria before opening his own spot, Chez Jolie, and launching the *Ingredienserna* podcast

Mikael Einarsson, Chef

Nose to Tail

With a dining scene as dynamic as Stockholm's, it pays to be an all-rounder, and Mikael Einarsson has that experience, leading several restaurants in different culinary styles. Inspired by an appetite for almost everything, he delivers tips for the best meatballs, herring plates, organic food markets and modern cocktails. He talks about getting closer to nature's spoils and the evolution of the local food scene with healthy competition spurring the top chefs

Frantzén
Norrmalm

Ekstedt
Östermalm

Rolfs Kök
Norrmalm

Lilla Ego
Vasastan

Sturehof
Östermalm

Tjoget
Södermalm

Babette
Vasastan

Teatern at Ringen Center
Södermalm

Pelikan
Södermalm

Tennstopet
Vasastan

What does Stockholm mean to you?

It has become my home and I really love this city. For me, Stockholm is one of the most beautiful cities I know. It's situated close to the water, the archipelago is close to the city and nature is just around the corner. And most of all, I love what's cooking!

The Stockholm dining scene has changed massively over the last decade. Why do you think this is?

Nordic cuisine made chefs and restaurants in Stockholm more comfortable in developing their own new style. I also think that Nordic cuisine took restaurants and chefs to a new level, where we could challenge each other. Knowing that the world was apparently watching us gave us self-confidence—it has inspired the new-generation chefs to do magic things. This, together with the Swedes getting more interested in food and spending more time and money at the restaurants, has created a new era—a dynamic and bubbling dining scene.

You cowrote Into the Wild, *an outdoor cookbook, and you like hunting. You obviously feel comfortable in nature. How do these go together, the outdoor guy and the chef/businessman?*

To be outdoors in nature can be just as inspiring for me as a restaurant visit. For me, hunting is a natural way of getting a better understanding of nature and having respect for the food that nature provides us with.

Speaking of the outdoors, what would you recommend for a quick getaway?

If you visit Stockholm for the first time, it would be almost criminal not to have a tour in the archipelago.

Apart from your own ventures, what other eateries are a must for visitors?

Frantzén is a restaurant with three Michelin stars. It's modern gastronomy with classic flavors. *Ekstedt*'s modern Nordic food cooked over an open fire earned it one Michelin star. *Rolfs Kök*, a modern institution of Stockholm gastronomy, produces European classic flavors in a casual but busy dining room. *Lilla Ego* is a contemporary version of Rolfs Kök, with modern tasty food. *Sturehof* is classic social dining with a mix of Swedish and French cooking. *Tjoget* is a place where you can stay all night in different parts of the locale. Good tasty food, a good wine bar and a good cocktail bar. *Babette* is a little place with tasty small plates and very good pizzas. And then there's *Teatern*—a food court with good modern fast food.

Given the size of Stockholm, it has quite a few decorated chefs. Is that inspiring or competitive?

For me it's competitive, but in an inspiring way. I would say that the climate between us is very friendly. In order to inspire each other and the producers, we get together on a regular basis to evaluate and discuss new produce and top-level breeders.

Are there any traditional Swedish restaurants one needs to visit?

I would recommend meatballs at *Pelikan*, the herring plate at *Sturehof*, or "Pelle Jansson" toast at *Tennstopet*.

We heard that there are hotels for bread dough in Stockholm. What's up with that?

(Laughs) That was several years ago. I don't know what the hipsters

Photo: Rolfkook

At Rolfs Kök in Norrmalm, diners can follow the preparation of their dish in the shiny, open kitchen

Vete-Katten
Norrmalm

Tössebageriet
Östermalm

Cadier Bar at Grand Hotel
Norrmalm

Spritmuseum
Djurgården

Fotografiska
Södermalm

Östermalms Saluhall
Östermalm

Hötorgshallen
Norrmalm

Paradiset
Södermalm

are up to right now.

Regarding the Swedish concept of "fika", can you explain and name your favorite spots?

Fika is when you have a coffee break with some cookies or buns—often cinnamon or cardamom. I would say the older generation fika at least twice a day. I normally have my fika at work, but my favorite spots in town would be *Vete-Katten* and *Tössebageriet*.

What bars would you recommend?

Cadier Bar at *Grand Hotel* for a classic cocktail with a view.

And what about museums?

We actually have some museums with very good restaurants: *Spritmuseum* (Spirit Museum) and *Fotografiska* (photography).

At what other food markets do you shop?

I would recommend *Östermalms Saluhall* and *Hötorgshallen*—classic food markets with fish, shellfish, meat, cheese and vegetables. And *Paradiset*, a market with organic food.

Is it really that difficult to buy a decent wine in Stockholm without spending your monthly salary?

Well, Stockholm is expensive, and taxes for wine and spirits are still very high. Right now, the positive thing for the customers is that competition between places keeps it down.

Above: Set in 18th-century naval buildings, the Spritmuseum offers the lowdown on Swedish booze and an acclaimed restaurant

Photos: 1) Spritmuseum

Vasastan

The Good Life

With charming greenery and 19th-century architecture, Vastastan (officially "Vasastaden") preserves its old-fashioned feel. Restaurants, galleries, antique dealers and vintage shops sit among several parks and architectural gems like the iconic city library

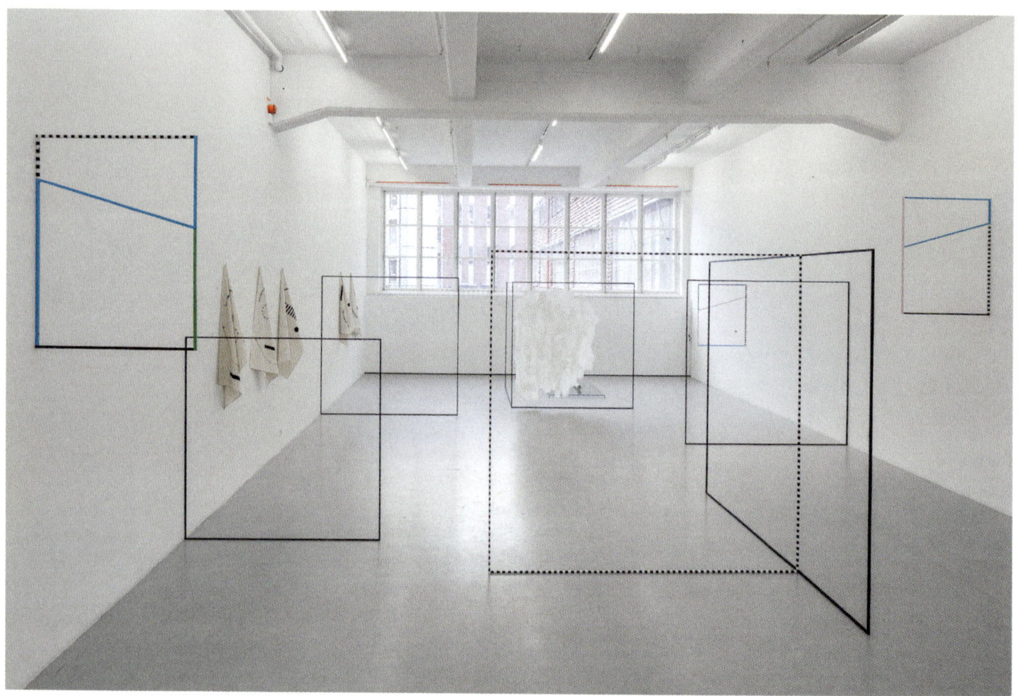

Photos: 1) Jean-Baptiste Beranger, 2) Klas Sjöberg LRF Media, 3) Acne, 4) Carla Orrego Veliz

Culture **Hanging Spaces**

In Vasastan beats the heart of Swedish contemporary art, concentrated on and around Hudiksvallsgatan street. On the ground floor of the transparent triangle on Torsgatan, *Bonniers Konsthall* is a modern art hub that offers free admission to all shows. Pop into *Sven-Harry's Museum* when strolling through Vasaparken. Get lost in a mirrored corridor or hit its rooftop to enjoy sculptures and a great view. For less constituted art, *Detroit Stockholm* brings together Swedish and foreign interdisciplinary artists. *Galleri Flach* forges connections between Nordic and African art. Since all these spaces and more lie within walking distance, good timing means you could jump from vernissage to vernissage in one night.
• Various locations, see Index, p.64, Vasastan

Food Sausage Party

Charismatic butcher brothers *Lennart & Bror* are carving up the city's meat scene with their stylish deli-cum-bistro in Vasastan. They attest to the provenance of the morsels in their store, with entrecôte from Lammhult specialized offerings like dry-aged on display. Light lunches are available on the premises—quality sausage in baguette is a popular option—and dinners can be enjoyed a few times a week. The Insta- and Facebook-friendly gents even hold a regular pub quiz—a fine chance to guzzle local beer and meet fellow meat-lovers.

• Lennart Och Bror, Birger Jarlsgatan 83 Vasastan, lennartochbror.se

Shop Bargain Designer

The *Acne Archive* is a mix of retail and outlet, with past collections at low prices to reward those with patience and a bit of luck. But the shop also attracts aficionados with one-off specials from the catwalks and a unique line of "recycled" pieces. Be sure to ask for other sizes or models from out back. Perhaps stop by *Acne Studios* in Norrmalm to check out the vaults of the former bank on the premises where a famous heist once took place. But the Archive is for stocking up without losing your own savings.

• Acne Archive, Torsgatan 53, Vasastan acnestudios.com

Food · Night Grandmother's Ruin

"Mysig," or cozy and comfortably homey, is a key concept in Swedish culture, and one that bar-cum-bistro and jazz café *Erlands* nails. It feels like visiting your long-lost Swedish grandparents' house—with the addition of a suave barman. Handpicked vintage decor fills the interior and a portrait of the owner's grandfather Erland watches over the all-age crowd. Fittingly, the menus are concealed inside time-worn novels: within them you'll find a list of outstanding cocktails like "Grandma's Temptation." Don't miss the regular live music nights.

• Erlands, Gästrikegatan 1, Vasastan, erlandsbar.se

Food Farm-to-Fika

The economical Swedish language has a separate expression for a sweet-treat coffee break: *fika*. For an award-winning fika experience, head to *Fosch Artisan Pâtisserie* on the edge of Vasastan. This charming café is the brainchild of a classically trained pastry chef and a former Swedish farmer who met at the famed Pascal Dupuy in Norway. The duo worked in restaurants around the world before opening two Fosch locations in Stockholm. The French and Swedish pastries are made with the freshest ingredients, including some the shop grows itself, for tasty treats that let the flavors speak for themselves.

• Fosch Artisan Pâtisserie, Birger Jarlsgatan 63, Vasastan, fosch.nu

Culture One for the Books

No architect has left such a mark on Stockholm's landscape as Gunnar Asplund. Among his works are the *Skogskyrkogården* graveyard, the interior of the majestic *Skandia* cinema and the *Stockholm Public Library—Stockholms Stadsbibliotek* for the natives—in Vasastan center. A great example of the late 1920s architectural style known as "Swedish Grace," this retro-futuristic structure is a worthy homage to literature. The mother of Pippi Longstocking, Astrid Lindgren, spent hours here. At nearly one hundred years old, the library is due for some upgrades—it will be closed for renovations through 2027.

• Stockholms Stadsbibliotek, Odengatan 63, Vasastan, biblioteket.stockholm.se

Shop Treasure Hunt

Vasastan may just have the city's highest concentration of antique stores. Explore the streets of Odengatan and Upplandsgatan to find old books and furniture at all styles and prices. On the latter, *Domino Antik* stands out with its curated focus on art deco and lamps from the 1930s to 1950s. Find such classics of Swedish design here as Stig Linberg's ashtrays, Lisa Larson's figurines or Kosta Boda glass. Just up the road is *Old Touch*—a mecca for vintage vultures. They sell goods on commission for private owners, which means you'll find anything from 19th-century lace to 1970s couture in addition to their private collection.

• Various locations, see Index, p.64, Vasastan

Photos: 1) David Jenison, 2) Staffan von Zeipel, 3) Old Touch, 4) Etoile, 5) David Jenison, 6) Carla Orrego Veliz

Food North Star

World travels often broaden a traveler's palate, but for the culinary minds behind *Etoile* (pictured), their global adventures ignited a spark of creative genius. Their aptly named restaurant (*étoile* is French for "star") offers a playful menu filled with unexpected flavor combinations and Instagram-worthy plating. For example, past dishes have included edible recreations of Banksy artwork and magic mushrooms. So far, Etoile has lived up to its name with a Michelin star, and the chefs recently earned another with *Celeste*, a sister restaurant in Södermalm with seasonal dishes and decor.
• Etoile, Norra Stationsgatan 51, Vasastan, restaurantetoile.se

Food Wrapper's Delight

Forget meatballs. For a real Swedish experience, head straight to *Matteus Kiosk & Grill* for a classic tunnbrödsrulle. This culinary Frankenstein combines hot dogs, mashed potatoes, creamy shrimp salad, ketchup, mustard, crispy onions, lettuce and spicy peppers, all snuggled together in a grilled flat-bread. This sounds like the brainchild of a college student with the munchies, but the combo is actually a 1960s Stockholm County creation with indigenous Sámi roots. It's also the go-to street food after clubbing and quite possibly the cipher key to IKEA's food section. The verdict? Anthony Bourdain said it best: "The most disgusting thing ever, and I love it."
• Matteus Kiosk & Grill, Vanadisvägen 13A, Vasastan

Food Contrasting Kitchens

Two sides of Stockholm sustenance can be found around the corner from each other in Vasastan. *Lilla Ego* is one of the stars of the city's gourmet Big Bang. The irreverent duo of super chefs (pictured) focuses on simple Swedish ingredients with a twist, serving their creations on IKEA plates and often working as waiters themselves. Book ahead or pop in late to watch the kitchen from the bar. *Tranan*, on the other hand, has been a mainstay of the traditional dining scene since 1929, with herring and mashed potatoes a staple on the menu since then. Duck into the cellar to have a nightcap at the atmospheric *Tranan Bar*.
• Various locations, see Index, p.64, Vasastan

Anna Camner, Artist

Prima Techniques

Anna Camner
Through her career, Anna's oil paintings have shifted between the figurative and the abstract. She is represented by the Loyal Gallery in Vasastan, and her works have been exhibited in London, Tokyo, Mumbai, Los Angeles and New York, alongside Stockholm

A graduate of the Royal Institute of Art in Stockholm, Anna Camner continues to find inspiration amongst the seasons of the city nearly 25 years later. She's perfected her alla prima paint style into expansions of surrealist oil artworks that explore the depths of psyche and emotion. She shares about the setting of her schooling, ideal spots for fashion hunts and where to find art and dine—with some places easier to nab a table than others

Photo: 1) Photo submitted by Anna Camner, 2) Restaurant Riche

Restaurant Riche has been a social meeting place for politicians, cultural figures, young hippies, old foxes and ordinary people since 1893

Moderna Museet
Skeppsholmen

ArkDes
Skeppsholmen

Your painting technique is described as a "wet-on-wet" style. Can you tell us a little bit about this and why you prefer this method?

For the past 25 years, I've painted alla prima or wet-on-wet, which is basically when wet paint never meets dry paint. What I find so extremely satisfying with this method is that it's possible to render the oil paint into endless variations in hue, and you can make really smooth transitions, which makes it really easy to play with volume.

You graduated from the Royal Institute of Art in Stockholm. What was it like studying there?

It's on a really beautiful island in the city center, called Skeppsholmen, where the school is located. It's next to the *Modern Art Museum*, or *Moderna Museet*, and the architecture museum, called *ArkDes*. So the environment is really beautiful and sometimes a little bit overwhelming. When I studied there in the 1990s, painting was kind of frowned upon. There were other trends in the art world at that time, but I'm sure that's changed.

Are there any specific ways in which Stockholm as a city influences your work?

For me, it's kind of good with the long dark winters. I can focus and there's not so much else going on, so it's good for me to be in the studio and paint. That's actually

Tegnérlunden
Norrmalm

Miyakodori
Norrmalm

Loyal Gallery
Vasastan

Babette
Vasastan

Nationalmuseum
Blasieholmen

Konst-ig
Södermalm

Restaurant Riche
Östermalm

Teatergrillen
Östermalm

really nice, I think, to be able to have that extended long period of time without distraction. A little bit of boredom can be kind of good for being creative, I think.

What is the art scene like in Stockholm?

Well, it's probably the same everywhere, but in Stockholm, I always felt it's quite individualistic, and I've been longing for more interaction with other artists and cooperating and more connection together. So a couple of years ago, my husband and I started an art platform called Black Iris that has 21 of Sweden's most established artists, and they're all represented by different galleries. I think it's the first platform in Sweden with established artists, and we create exhibitions in very central, but also rough, locations in Stockholm, where art hasn't been shown before. We make quite ambitious exhibitions in short pop-ups.

In what neighborhood do you reside? What are some of your favorite local spots to frequent when you are living through your normal day?

We live in Norrmalm, which is the center, and there's a cute park nearby called *Tegnérlunden*, which has a little pond where little kids can swim. There is a nice Japanese restaurant close by called *Miyakodori*. It has really nice karaage.

Your series "Places to Be" is currently on exhibit with Loyal Gallery *on Odengaten. Any recommendations for places nearby after someone sees the show?*

They are the only gallery in that area, and there's a nice restaurant close by called *Babette*. They have natural wines, nice food, and a nice atmosphere. It's more relaxed, but you have to book months ahead.

When you're looking to get inspired, what are some galleries, museums, parks or exhibits you frequent?

For me it's mostly music that's inspiration. I also really enjoy seeing medieval Flemish paintings, but there's not so much of that in Stockholm, sadly. There are a few in the *Nationalmuseum*, which is a beautiful museum, but not anywhere else really. I also like to go to a bookshop in Södermalm called *Konst-ig* that has really nice art books.

Any fun places for a night out on the town or meal for a special occasion? Bars, venues or special occasion spots?

Restaurant Riche. For a long time they've had an art profile. I know internationally, art exhibitions in restaurants and bars are not super prestigious, but Riche has a long tradition of showing the top artists like Karin Mamma Andersson or Jens Fänge. All the biggest Swedish artists basically have shown in Riche and *Teatergrillen*. Teatergrillen is in the same building, two different restaurants, but they have the same art director that is curating. His name is Carl Carboni, and he's done this for so many years. The food is nice, and they change exhibits every couple of months.

When you want to escape city life, where do you go?

Well, I really like city life. I'm not so much for the countryside. I don't understand why anyone would ever want to not be in the city. But when I get really tired of Stockholm, I go to a bigger city like New York or Tokyo or Paris.

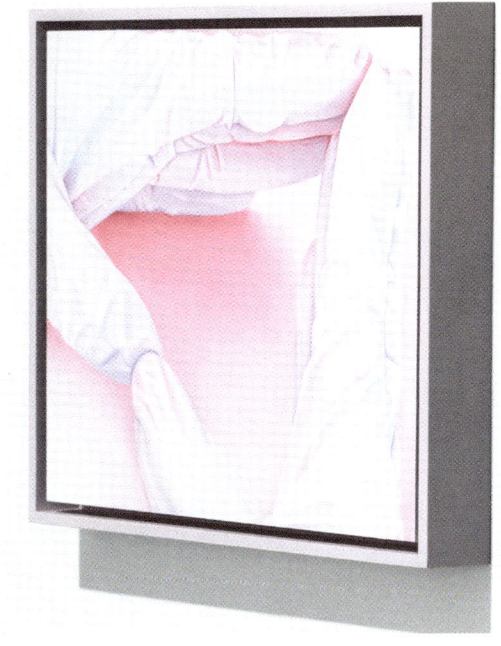

Anna's artwork hangs on display in Loyal Gallery

The Forumist Södermalm

Any particularly unique shops or markets you'd like to recommend or mention?

Yes, there's a divine little shop in Södermalm called *The Forumist*. They have a curated selection of emerging young new designers, like fashion designers and jewelry and also some art. Some of the designers are Keta Gutmane, who is Latvian, and Christina Prieth, who is French. Lots of really super nice Swedish and international brands. They have everything anyone would ever need. It's on Hökens gata in Slussen.

Your next solo exhibition is coming up at Ståhl Collection, Norrköping, Sweden. Any clues as to what this series will be or what your inspiration is?

I will show a series of abstract and figurative paintings. I call the exhibition "The Weight of Light." It's basically about the emotional intensity of seeing things as they are. I try to hide the obvious and reveal the hidden.

Axel Boman, Musician

Upbeat

Axel Boman
Stockholm's own Axel Boman has been making waves since his 2010 breakout track "Purple Drank" on DJ Koze's Pampa Records. From GAFFA and Swedish Grammy nominations to co-founding the influential Studio Barnhus label and studio, Boman is a driving force in the house music scene. He's lit up stages at Coachella, Burning Man and Sónar while growing his vast collection of releases, collaborations and production credits

When he's not performing on stage or immersed in the studio, Axel Boman soaks up inspiration from his hometown surroundings—whether it's the best late-night haunts, traditional Swedish kitchens or underground parties. Through Boman's eyes, see a local's perspective on the city's party scene and the experiences that infuse his music with its distinctive *joie de vivre*.

Photo: LIFTD x Axel Boman

Trädgården
Södermalm

Musikaliska Kvarteret
Norrmalm

Slakthuset
Johanneshov

Berns Hotel
Norrmalm

Did your upbringing influence you to become an artist?

Yeah, kind of. My mom is an actress and my dad is a scenographer. I grew up in theaters when I was a kid. My mom was employed at the National Theater in Stockholm for all her life. Most people grow up in surroundings that say you have to get an education and a nine-to-five job. I am the perfect mix of my parents. I love to create a crazy show but I do not like to be the center of attention.

And how did you end up becoming a DJ and producer?

My brother is six years older than me and grew up with the first wave of acid house. He started going to Sweden's first raves and often to London. His records became my first records when he stopped caring about them. I wanted to learn how to scratch, so I attended a DJ school in a youth center. After that I played for friends at parties, went a little bit to raves and learned about the Stockholm scene of the late 1990s. As this was before the internet, I went to record stores to meet guys interested in music. It was that easy. If you liked breakdance, you went to that corner in town. If you liked techno, you went to this store. After school I was accepted to Gothenburg's art academy and then met Petter Nordkvist and Kornél Kovács. It was a great environment to start making music.

And then you moved back to Stockholm. Why?

I came back for family and friends. Not for Stockholm itself. Here, many people are "too cool" for Stockholm and think other places are cooler. I don't like this—Stockholm is not Berlin, and why should it be? It's a quiet, beautiful city that's expensive and has a real long winter. Sweden used to be famous for its social democracy and the equality of society. But this has gone. Now we live in a cold environment where the right wing movement is getting really strong and the big parties collaborate with them. Like in many parts of Europe.

But is the nightlife of Stockholm still liberal?

The nightlife has never been better. We've suddenly caught up with the rest of Europe. We have great clubs and parties with good lineups and music, every weekend. This was never the case when I was young, and it's a good thing.

Can you name us some of your favorite spots?

You have the *Trädgården*, a great outdoor place with great line-ups. It's called Under Bron during winter because "trädgården" means "the garden." In summertime it becomes this big open-air thing, open all week. It's beautiful. You have places to eat and it's under a bridge. So, even if it's raining a little bit, you're fine. This is south of the center. Then you have *Musikaliska*, quite a new place. They also have a courtyard, and it's really nice to hang out there. It's a mixture of bar and club. They also make very ambitious bookings. *Slakthuset* is an industrial club more into techno. And there's *Berns*, where I used to have a residency. But another important thing for nightlife in Stockholm is the bar life. There are so many great DJs in Stockholm that never play outside of the city. They have great selections so the quality of music—even if you go just to a bar to hang

East
Östermalm

Riche
Östermalm

Tennstopet
Vasastan

Lilla Ego
Vasastan

Acne Archive
Vasastan

Record Mania
Södermalm

Snickars Records
Södermalm

out—is super. I also go a lot to *East* or *Riche*.

And what makes them special?

Each is different. *Riche* is really fancy and they have good DJs. There you can order oysters and champagne and listen to great music. All the bars close at 2 or 3am. But as soon as springtime hits town, rave season kicks off and you have outdoor parties all the time. To find out where they are, go to the bars I mentioned and ask—I'm sure you'll end up with a good dance.

And where do you find the sustenance for such a night?

There are many good restaurants. I always take DJ Koze to *Tennstopet*. He never wants to leave. It is an all-Swedish place. You eat meatballs and drink beer. All the waiters wear white shirts and it looks really old. Everybody who works there is old and unfriendly (laughs). They are super professional and seem to be doing everything effortlessly. You are super looked after, despite the unfriendly style. It's the best place for eating typical Swedish. For great modern Scandinavian cuisine you have *Lilla Ego*—a really fancy place. It's almost Michelin level. You can't make reservations. You just show up and sit down on long tables; the food is fantastc.

Would you say Stockholm is overpriced?

For natives I wouldn't say so. But if you come with a budget, you'll be surprised by the cost of a beer. Oh, and make sure you get taxis from the right companies: Taxi Stockholm, Taxi Kurir and Taxi 020. Take one of them and nobody else.

What would you do on a weekend in Stockholm?

I'd go to my girlfriend who works at the *Acne Archives*, downtown. It is a store where everybody interested in fashion should go. They sell samples from old collections you do not get anywhere else. I live in Gröndall, near Vinterviken—a great park. You can see islands, water and wildlife. And this is walking distance to Södermalm, the picturesque part of Stockholm. Here you have many cool cafés, bars, restaurants and clothing stores of young local designers. Also, there you can take a boat and go out of town to an island. That's great too!

Do you also look for music in Södermalm?

Always. I go to two record stores: *Record Mania* is world famous for disco, soul, rare grooves, old hip-hop and afro records. But they have their price. Then you have *Snickars Records*, with a great, great second-hand selection. You can spend a day in there.

And how's park life in Stockholm?

Since Stockholm has many islands connected by bridges, there are parks everywhere. Just follow the water, and you'll find one. There are bigger parks like the Royal Park in the center and on Södermalm there's Vitabergspraken with nice hills and great views. But you can't drink beer outside. That's important to know! I got fined once. Also important to know is that in Stockholm you can only buy alcohol in state-owned stores. So I'd recommend going first to one of these stores and stocking your fridge with less expensive drinks to drink before hitting the bars.

Östermalm's East is a specialist in Asian fusion cuisine and large circles

Katarina Ölkafé
Södermalm

Hotel Hornsgatan
Södermalm

Could you share any Stockholm secrets not to be found in regular travel guides?

Check out *Katarina Ölkafé*, a rustic, old-style beer café. It looks like it's from the 1920s. They only serve beer and sandwiches. It's in the quite nice Sofo neighborhood—its name means "south of Folkungagatan street." And I always tell people to check out *Hotel Hornsgatan*. It's a lovely place that's good for your wallet, in walking distance to good bars, restaurants, historical places and so on. It's perfectly located! In Stockholm it's easy to get around. The metro is super easy. Or you can rent a bike everywhere.

Editors' Picks

Stockholm Syndrome

Cork Walkers

Launched in Stockholm by three friends—Jonathan Hirschfeld, Charlie Hedin, and former Acne Studios designer Max Schiller—Eytys is a clean-cut unisex sneaker label. It's informed by street culture, and the shoes are unique for their cork-filled platform. The key styles are good looking and functional—you can't get more Swedish than that.
• Eytys Doja shoes, eytys.com

Perfect Praline

Ejes have been melting chocolate, whipping truffles and kneading marzipan for nearly one hundred years. Using the same process they developed in 1923, they make their sweets on site in their stores. A little bite of praline is perfected for almost two days, but enjoyed in a matter of seconds.
• Ejes Choklad, ejeschoklad.se

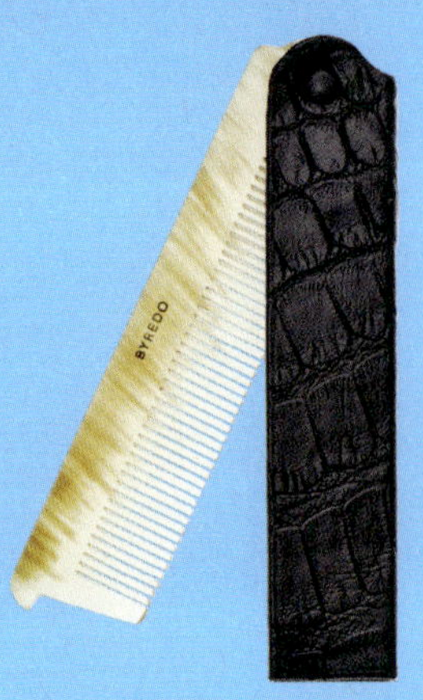

Combing the City

Ben Gorham used to be a pro basketball player; now he's a low-key genius in the beauty world with his Stockholm brand Byredo. Inspired by memory and travel, he's developed a handsome collection of scents, soaps and accessories—including this leather-cased pocket comb, which gets better looking with each use, just like you. Available in store only.
• Byredo pocket comb, byredo.com

Books

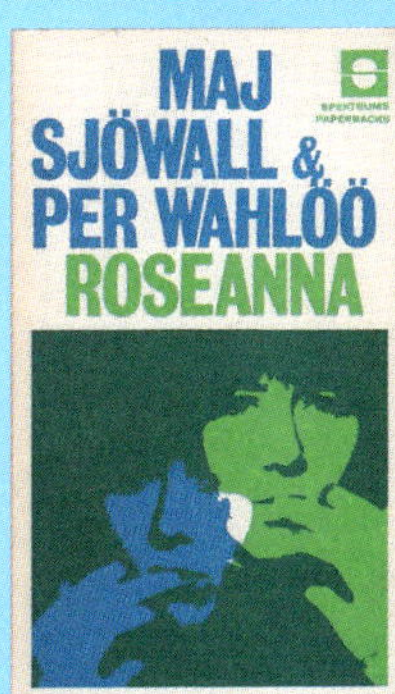

Roseanna, A Martin Beck Novel
• Maj Sjöwall and Per Wahlöö, 1965

The father of Nordic noir, detective Martin Beck was likely inspiration for Mankell, Larsson and co. *Roseanna* is the first of ten novels written in alternating chapters by the husband and wife team.

New Collected Poems
• Tomas Tranströmer, 2011

The late 2011 Nobel laureate was dubbed the "buzzard poet" owing to his soaring perspective. Passing from nature poetry to more personal themes, Tranströmer's collection is available in a prize-winning translation by Robin Fulton.

Karlsson on the Roof
• Astrid Lindgren

Lindgren's tale about a young boy's little flying friend won her fans around the world, especially in the former USSR, where rebellious Karlsson struck a chord. See Stockholm from his view with Takvandring Rooftop Tours.

Films

Together
• Lukas Moodysson, 2000

This tragicomic depiction of a 1970s Stockholm hippy commune bleeds beyond Swedish borders. Diverse people combat loneliness while seeking love and meaning in a film equal parts painful and charming.

Summer with Monika
• Ingmar Bergman, 1953

Lesser known but hugely influential among the master's oeuvre, this is the story of two working-class teenagers who flee Stockholm on an amorous adventure. It influenced the cliché of Sweden as an erotic paradise.

Let the Right One In
• Tomas Alfredson, 2008

In a grim Stockholm suburb, a lonely boy befriends a girl with a bloody secret.... This alternative take on the vampire genre is one of Sweden's most compelling recent exports.

Music

The World Is Saved
• by Stina Nordenstam, 2004

Dreamy, melancholic and intimate: Nordenstam's songs of love and loss reflect Sweden's changing seasons. *The World Is Saved* is a master class in alt-pop by the reclusive singer-songwriter, who hasn't performed live for years.

Total
• by Baba Stiltz, 2014

Stockholm's most refreshing dance music in recent years comes out of Studio Barnhus. The label, run by Axel Boman and friends, offers a colorful and cheery variety of house music—and this debut album is solid proof.

Ahh! Monica!
• by Monica Zetterlund, 1962

Sweden's beloved jazz singer enjoyed a successful career for almost 50 years. Her second album, recorded with influential band leader Georg Riedel, opens with "Sakta vi gå genom stan," a lush tribute to her hometown Stockholm.

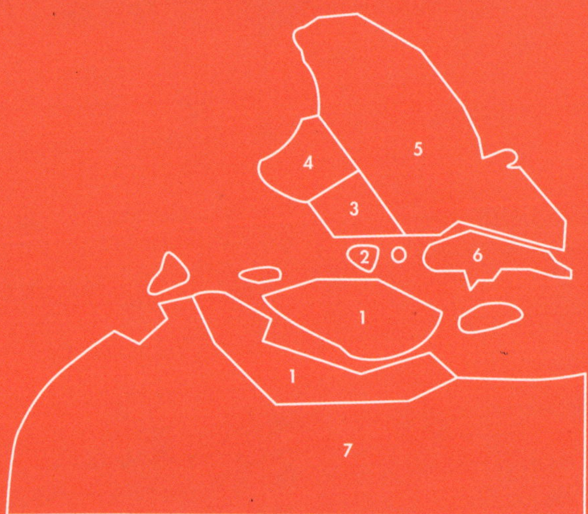

Districts

1 Södermalm
2 Gamla Stan
3 Norrmalm
4 Vasastan
5 Östermalm
6 Djurgården
7 Söderort

Ⓐ Art
Ⓒ Culture
Ⓕ Food
Ⓝ Night
Ⓞ Outdoors
Ⓢ Shop

1/ Södermalm

Aplace
Götgatan 36
+46 8 643 31 10
aplace.com → p. 18

Årstaviken/
Tanto Beach
Tantolunden Park
→ p. 31 Ⓞ

Bio Rio Cinema
Hornstull Strand 3
+46 8 669 95 00
biorio.se → p. 31 Ⓒ

Celeste
Torkel
Knutssonsgatan 24
+46 08 502 769 61
celesterestaurant.se
→ p. 53 Ⓕ

Deadwood Studios
Bondegatan 48
+46 70 866 18 66
deadwoodstudios.com
→ p. 18 Ⓢ

Debaser Strand
Hornstulls strand 4
debaser.se → p. 24 Ⓝ

Dovas Bar
Hornsgatan 90
+46 8 429 92 10
→ p. 32 Ⓝ

Eriksdalsbadet
Hammarby Slussväg 20
→ p. 8 Ⓞ

Färgfabriken
Lövholmsbrinken 1
+46 8 64 50 707
fargfabriken.se
→ p. 20 Ⓒ

The Forumist
Hökens gata 8
theforumist.com
→ p. 57 Ⓢ

Fotografiska
Stadsgårdshamnen 22
+46 8 50 90 05 00
fotografiska.eu
→ p. 9, 23, 24, 25, 48
Ⓒ Ⓕ

Gamla Amsterdam
Hornsgatan 39A
Södermalm
+46 73 342 37 21
gamla-amsterdam.se
→ p. 15 Ⓕ Ⓢ

Grandpa
Södermannagatan 21
+46 10 516 44 80
grandpastore.com
→ p. 18 Ⓢ

Hommage
Krukmakargatan 22
+46 8 658 42 50
hommage.se
→ p. 15 Ⓕ

Hotel Hornsgatan
Hornsgatan 66B
+46 8 658 29 01
biorio.se → p. 61 Ⓒ

Judits
Hornsgatan 75
+46 8 84 45 10
judits.se → p. 20 Ⓢ

Katarina Ölkafé
Katarina Bangata 27
→ p. 61 Ⓕ

Konst-ig
Åsögatan 124
+46 8 20 45 20
konstigbooks.com
→ p. 15, 56 Ⓢ

Lundbergs Konditori
Sjöbjörnsvägen 2
+46 8 645 20 34
lundbergskonditori.se
→ p. 15 Ⓕ

Mullvaden Antikvariat
Torkel Knutssons-
gatan 31 → p. 32 Ⓢ

Nitty Gritty
Krukmakargatan
24–26
+46 8 658 24 40
nittygrittystore.com
→ p. 18 Ⓢ

Nook
Åsögatan 176
+46 8 702 12 22
nookrestaurang.se
→ p. 19 Ⓕ

Nū
Teatern Ringen
Götgatan 132
nusthlm.com
→ p. 10 Ⓢ

Nudie Jeans
Skånegatan 75
+46 10 151 57 15
nudiejeans.com
→ p. 18 Ⓢ

Orionteatern
Katarina Bangata 77
orionteatern.se
→ p. 31 Ⓒ

Östgötakällaren
Östgötagatan 41
+46 8 643 22 40
osgotakallaren.se
→ p. 32 Ⓕ

Papercut
Krukmakargatan 24
papercutshop.se
→ p. 18 Ⓢ

Paradiset
Brännkyrkagatan 62
+46 8 613 36 00
paradiset.com
→ p. 48 Ⓢ

Pelikan
Blekingegatan 40
+46 8 55 60 90 90
pelikan.se → p. 24, 32, 46

POP Stockholm
Åsögatan 140
+46 8 64 24 500
popstockholm.se
→ p. 18 Ⓢ

Raamen
Teatern Ringen
Götgatan 132
+46 08 206 125
raamen.se → p. 10 Ⓢ

Record Mania
Östgötagatan 2
+46 8 600 03 24
recordmania.se
→ p. 60 Ⓢ

2/Gamla Stan

3/Norrmalm

4/Vasastan

5/Östermalm

East
Stureplan 13
+46 8 611 49 59
east.se → p. 60 Ⓕ

Ekstedt
Humlegårdsgatan 17
+46 8 611 12 10
ekstedt.nu → p. 46 Ⓕ

Filmhuset
Borgvägen 1
+46 8 665 11 00
filminstitutet.se
→ p. 6 Ⓒ

Galleri Flach
Karlavägen 9
+46 8 661 13 99
galleriflach.com
→ p. 50 Ⓒ

Galeri Nordenhake
Lutzengatan 1
+46 8 21 18 92
nordenhake.com
→ p. 16 Ⓒ

Jacksons
Sibyllegatan 53
+46 70 545 40 49
jacksons.se → p. 10 Ⓢ

Larsen Warner
Sturegatan 28
+46 8 667 21 90
larsenwarner.com
→ p. 23, 24 Ⓒ

Lisa Elmqvist
Nybrogatan 31
+46 8 553 404 00
lisaelmqvist.se
→ p. 10 Ⓕ

Nordiska Galleriet
Nybrogatan 11
+46 8 442 83 60
nordiskagalleriet.se
→ p. 26, 28, 29 Ⓢ

Östermalms Saluhall
Östermalmsgatan 31
ostermalmshallen.se
→ p. 10, 29, 48

Riche
Birger Jarlsgatan 4
+46 8 545 035 60
riche.se
→ p. 25, 56, 60 Ⓕ

Skultuna
Grev Turegatan 18
+46 8 545 835 55
skultuna.com
→ p. 27, 28 Ⓢ

Strandvägen 1
Strandvägen 1
+46 8 66 38 000
strandvagen1.se
→ p. 24 Ⓕ

Sturehof
Stureplan 2
+46 8 440 57 30
sturehof.com → p. 46 Ⓕ

Svenskt Tenn
Strandvägen 5
+46 8 67 01 600
svenskttenn.se
→ p. 10, 26, 27, 28 Ⓢ

Teatergrillen
Nybrogatan 3
+46 8 545 035 65
teatergrillen.se
→ p. 56 Ⓕ

Tössebageriet
Karlavägen 77
+46 8 662 24 30
tosse.se → p. 48 Ⓕ

6/ Djurgården

Liljevalchs Konsthall
Djurgårdsvägen 60
+46 8 508 313 30
liljevalchs.se → p. 28 Ⓒ

Skansen Museum
Djurgårdsslätten 49–51
+46 8 44 28 000
skansen.se → p. 25 Ⓒ

Spritmuseum
Djurgårdsstrand 9
+46 8 121 313 00
spritmuseum.se/en
→ p. 24, 48 Ⓒ

Vasa Museum
Galärvarvsvägen 14
+46 8 51 95 48 00
vasamuseet.se
→ p. 25 Ⓒ

7/Söderort

Kaffé Express Colombia
Hökarängsplan 5
+46 8 777 38 11
→ p. 21 Ⓕ

Konsthall C
Cigarrvägen 14
+46 8 60 47 708
konsthallc.se → p. 21 Ⓒ

Skogskyrkogården
Sockenvägen
+46 8 508 301 00
skogskyrkogarden.se
→ p. 16, 52 Ⓞ

Slakthuset
Slakthusgatan 6
→ p. 59 Ⓝ

Other

2 Little Spoons
Vattenledningsvägen 42B
+46 0721 90 89 21
2littlespoons.com
→ p. 20 Ⓢ

Aloë
Svartlösavägen 52
+46 73 154 41 51
aloerestaurant.se
→ p. 8 Ⓕ

ArkDes
Exercisplan 4
+46 8 520 235 00
arkdes.se → p. 55 Ⓐ

Artipelag
Artipelagstigen 1
+46 8 570 130 00
artipelag.se → p. 11 Ⓒ

Etoile
Norra Stationsgatan 51
+46 8 10 10 70
restaurantetoile.se
→ p. 53 Ⓕ

Frantzén
Klara Norra kyrkogata 26
+46 8 20 85 80
restaurantfrantzen.com
→ p. 8, 46 Ⓕ

Gaia Matbar
Vattenledningsvägen 44
+46 76 021 45 11
gaiamatbar.se
→ p. 20 Ⓕ

Kollektivet
Hökarängsplan 7
+46 8 428 457 79
kollektivetihokis.se
→ p. 21 Ⓕ

Moderna Museet
Exercisplan 4
+46 8 520 235 00
modernamuseet.se
→ p. 55 Ⓐ

Nationalmuseum
Södra Blasieholmshamnen 2
+46 8 519 543 00
nationalmuseum.se
→ p. 56 Ⓐ

Nystekt Strömming
Kornhamnstorg 1
+46 73 971 92 47
→ p. 19 Ⓕ

Saltsjöbadens Friluftsbad
Torben Gruts väg 8, Saltsjöbaden → p. 8 Ⓞ

Smedsuddsbadet
Smeduddsvägen 1
→ p. 8 Ⓞ

Yasuragi
Hamndalsvägen 8, Saltsjö-Boo
+46 8 74 76 100
yasuragi.se → p. 25 Ⓞ

Building a House Where You Can Sleep and Eat

Fredrik Carlström

I was born in Stockholm and spent the first half of my life there. Since moving to New York in 2000, I have been in a polyamorous, long-distance relationship with Stockholm. Travel is at least as much about our internal state of mind as it is about external sights, so returning home always brings up a lot of feelings for me.

In literature, it's often said there are only two original stories. The first one, the "A Person Goes on a Journey," focuses on the protagonist venturing out from their familiar environment into the unknown. This journey often represents a quest for knowledge, self-discovery or a mission to achieve a specific goal. The protagonist faces challenges, overcomes obstacles and is usually transformed by their experiences. Classic examples include Homer's *The Odyssey*, an ancient epic that follows Odysseus as he leaves home to fight in the Trojan War and makes his long, adventurous journey back to Ithaca. In J.R.R. Tolkien's *The Hobbit*, Bilbo Baggins leaves the comfort of his home to join a group of dwarves on a quest to reclaim their homeland from the dragon Smaug. When Alice tumbles down a rabbit hole in Lewis Carroll's *Alice's Adventures in Wonderland*, she leaves her mundane world behind to enter the fantastical world of Wonderland.

In contrast, the other archetype, "A Stranger Comes to Town," revolves around the idea of an outsider entering a new place. Their arrival disrupts the status quo, catalyzing events and changes in the lives of those they encounter. In *The Great Gatsby* by F. Scott Fitzgerald, Jay Gatsby, the enigmatic millionaire, plays the role of the stranger whose arrival sets the plot in motion, revealing the tensions and dynamics of the social circle in West Egg. In Bram Stoker's *Dracula*, the arrival of Count Dracula in England brings with it a series of mysterious and terrifying events, impacting the lives of those he encounters. In Harper Lee's classic novel *To Kill a Mockingbird*, Boo Radley is the mysterious figure whose actions and presence significantly affect events and perspectives in the small town of Maycomb.

New landscapes act as mirrors for our thoughts and emotions; they can change how we see ourselves, not just how we see the destination. One of travel's greatest gifts is its ability to jolt us into looking at the world—ours and others'—with fresh eyes. When we have grown numb to our surroundings, even the mundane can become remarkable when viewed through the lens of a traveler's curiosity. Each new journey can illuminate aspects of our own personality. By engaging with the unfamiliar, we learn more about our preferences, fears, and values—and return home changed in ways both subtle and profound.

The Sum of Its Parts

To me, magic happens when a group of things—or people—interacting with one another creates something different or greater than when they act in isolation. That's why I was so excited when, in the fall of 2020, I was invited to open a hotel in Stockholm.

There are trends in everything, and many hotels and real estate developments promote the architect or interior designer. Personally, I've long wondered what would happen if a hotel were restaurateur driven. To take all the knowledge from hospitality—the art of welcoming and creating atmosphere—and apply that to the whole guest experience. To put people first and let design follow. Build a space where locals feel at home and that automatically becomes the most interesting place for curious travelers.

It's the Lust for Life That Binds People Together

In Swedish culture, the term *stadshotell* carries a certain nostalgia—an echo of bourgeois elegance, traditional dining rooms with white tablecloths and classic service. Traditionally found in small and medium-sized towns, often planted right in the central square, stadshotell first emerged in the 19th century as important social hubs that hosted travelers and business meetings, parties and formal gatherings. Different social classes—businessmen, local dignitaries, traveling merchants, the occasional cultural or political figure—crossed paths in these stately hotels.

Over generations, some stadshotell have thrived while others have fallen from grace. Modern renovations often blend historical charm with contemporary comfort, revitalizing that old-world allure. In many ways, a stadshotell is the Nordic cousin to Europe's grand hotels or railway hotels, though it remains more down-to-earth, more local. You can almost sense a literary character perched at the bar, soaking in the slightly faded splendor. Or recall Swedish author Fritiof Nilsson Piraten's *Bombi Bitt och jag*, where a small-town stadshotell, the fictional Hotell Horn, is the backdrop for roguish adventures, comedic intrigue and the eccentric mix of people who gather there.

Some iconic real-life examples include Stadshotellet i Kalmar, a central landmark for much of the 20th century, and Stadshotellet i Lund, a meeting spot for academics and businesspeople alike. Ystad Stadshotell, with its historical atmosphere, even served as a filming location for Henning Mankell's *Wallander* series. Through all these variations, the stadshotell remains a symbol of Swedish hospitality—bridging past and present, elegance and approachability.

A House Where You Can Eat and Sleep

For me, Stockholm Stadshotell is a love letter to that tradition and to the people who make Stockholm great. Treating the house as carefully as one would treat an expensive ingredient while cooking, we let the Arts and Crafts Movement be a source of inspiration and worked with artists, designers and craftspeople to create our version of the classic family-run or owner-operated inn.

A place where locals are drawn in by the comfort of good food and good company; where travelers feel the authentic pulse of the city through its people, rather than the hum of a generic lobby that has been "curated" to death. In that sense, it's like an art school: a melting pot of ideas, personalities and the kind of beauty and truth that make a city feel like home.

Stockholm always be my first love. By moving away, I gained new perspectives and grew as a person. With the opening of this new hotel, I am able to bring some of that back home, and I hope its presence will affect events and people in a positive way.

Fredrik Carlström is a creative director, entrepreneur, investor and partner of the Stockholm Stadshotell, specializing in projects that span deep tech (like quantum computing company SEEQC) and place-making (like Stockholm Stadshotell and Alma). Originally from Stockholm, he lives in New York with his daughter.

Image by Renata Zandonadi, courtesy of Stockholm Stadshotell.

Available from LOST iN

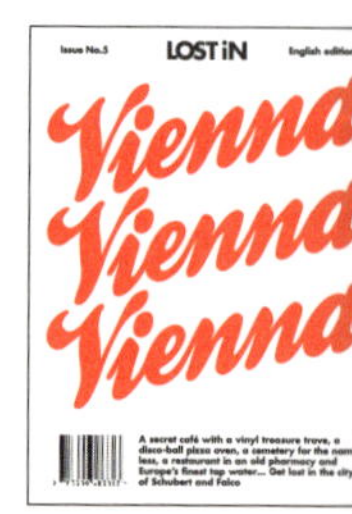

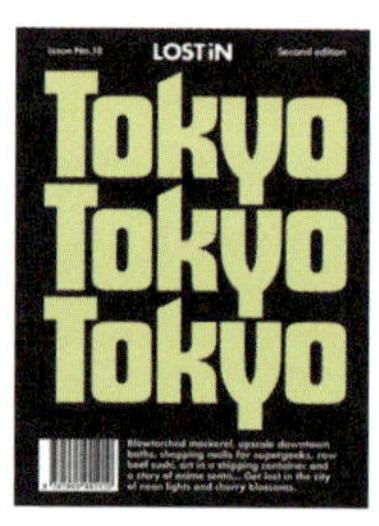

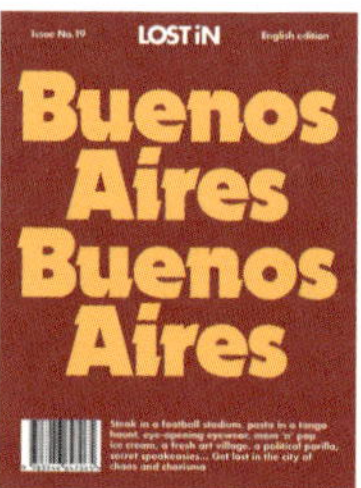

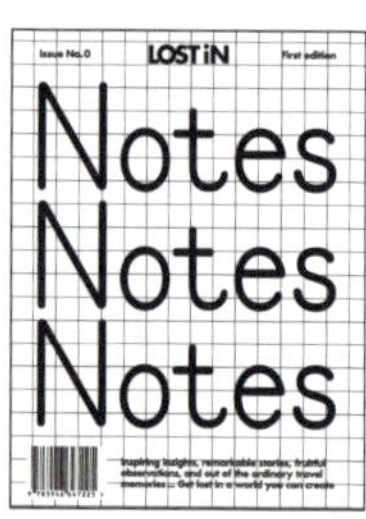

LOSTIN.COM